A CARDIFF CENTURY

A CARDIFF CENTURY

A capital city for Wales

Brian Lee

DB
PUBLISHING

First published in Great Britain by
The Breedon Books Publishing Company Limited
Unit 3, The Parker Centre, Mansfield Road, Derby, DE21 4SZ
2004.

This paperback edition published in Great Britain in 2013 by DB Publishing,
an imprint of JMD Media Ltd

ISBN 978-1-78091-338-4

Printed and bound in the UK by Copytech (UK) Ltd Peterborough

Contents

Author's Acknowledgements

For allowing me access to the *Western Mail & Echo's* vast archive of pictures, and for writing the foreword, I would first of all like to thank the *Echo's* editor Alastair Milburn. I am also indebted to the chief librarian at Thomson House, Tony Woolway, and his staff, namely Rob Mager, Edwina Turner and Maria Jorge who were most helpful. Another Thomson House employee who must take some credit for this book is assistant editor Margaret O'Reilly, who found a publisher for my first Cardiff book when she wrote an article about me back in 1996.

Special thanks go to Stewart Williams for writing the introduction and whose series of *Cardiff Yesterday* books has been an inspiration. Others I need to thank are those people who loaned me photographs and they are Tony Blood, Bernard Driscoll, Derek Carder, Gerald May, Tom Cronin, Marion Jenkins, Ray Impney, Russell Harvey, Christine Ashley, David Davies, Valerie Beames, Mrs A. Bannister, Mrs B. Morgan, Mrs Evans, Mrs Mary Clay, Phyllis Shergold, John Morgan and James Shaughnessy of David Morgan Ltd and the Capitol Centre Marketing and Promotions Manager Nia Williams, Centre Manager Jeff Wilson, and Administrator Sandra James.

I also need to thank the staff of the Central Cardiff Library Local Studies Department for answering my queries and those people who loaned me photographs which I was unable to use. Finally, I ask forgiveness from anyone who may feel they have been omitted from these acknowledgements.

Foreword

Every major milestone deserves a lasting memorial – and what better way of leaving your mark on history than in print?

So when it came to celebrating Cardiff's 100th birthday as a city and 50th anniversary as the capital of Wales, the historic year just had to be recorded in words and pictures.

Asked for help by Cardiff historian Brian Lee in compiling a special birthday tribute to the city he was born and brought up in, I was delighted to give him access to our vast library of photographs and stories at the *South Wales Echo*.

This remarkable and very readable book is the product of Brian's nine-month labour of love, in which he takes us on a fascinating journey through time, charting the many changing faces of Cardiff from the moment it was granted its city status in 1905 by King Edward VII, to the modern, technological and vibrant European capital in which we live, work and visit today.

Who would have known, for instance, that the world-famous Cardiff Arms Park rugby ground had been the venue in the 1920s for that woolly sporting spectacle... of sheep dog trials!

How many remember the sea of faces that filled Duke Street and Castle Street in 1947 to witness that historic moment when the Marquess of Bute handed over his ancestral home of Cardiff Castle and all its grounds to the people of Cardiff?

And who could forget the screaming hordes outside the old Capitol Theatre in Queen Street (now the Capitol Shopping Centre) when the Beatles came to play in 1964, or the winter of 1979 when the River Taff burst its banks and transformed Canton and Riverside into one vast lake?

All those memories – and much, much more – help to make up the extraordinary and meticulous collection that is *A Cardiff Century: A Capital City for Wales*.

The *Echo*, of course, has played a starring role in chronicling the everyday life of Cardiff throughout its first 100 years as a city, and we are proud to be closely associated with this gem of a book.

Having lived in Cardiff for all but the first couple of months of my life, I know what a very special city and capital it is.

I am confident that you will not fail to enjoy this magical and memorable book. It's destined to become a part of our great city's history…

Alastair Milburn
Editor
South Wales Echo

Introduction

In the inter-war years Cardiff was known as the 'City Beautiful'. Today it has much else to be proud of – the Bay developments, which have transformed an area of depressing dereliction into one of the best examples of urban regeneration in Europe, and the splendid Millennium Stadium, which thanks to television, has brought international recognition to the city.

The skyline too has been altered with modern office blocks, luxury flats and multi-storey car parks replacing old familiar places which are still fondly remembered by septuagenarians like myself. Cinemas and at least one arcade have been sacrificed to make way for ultra-modern shopping malls. All this has, of course, created jobs and boosted the economy.

But this latest book from the indefatigable Brian Lee is not concerned with present-day Cardiff. It is all about nostalgia, 'a sentimental yearning for the past' – and something I am familiar with through the *Cardiff Yesterday* series, published between 1980–2000. Every one of the 36 volumes containing some 7,500 photographs was a journey down memory lane.

Memory is such a precious thing. In 1985 I received a letter from Dr D.S. Campbell of the League of Friends of St Mary's and Llandough Day Hospitals. He wrote 'Our occupational therapists have noted the therapeutic response which your books provoke in patients when they see photographs of scenes familiar to them in the past.'

This gratifying reaction was repeated many times over during the 20-year life of the series and was an additional bonus to the pleasure of compiling and publishing the books.

As Brian will readily admit, the fun is in the gathering of the pictures, many of them seeing light of day for the first time as precious family albums have been generously made available to us. Then there is the thrill of meeting for the first time sporting idols from the past. Who could fail to be excited at the prospect of meeting Jack Petersen, the boxing giant of the 1930s who had half of Cardiff glued to their wireless sets for his epic battles with Walter Neusel. It was the German who denied Jack his crack at a world title when he badly injured the Cardiff man's eye.

The couple of hours spent in Jack's company chatting about his career and admiring items of Petersen memorabilia will always remain in my memory. A decade before Jack's exploits in the ring, Cardiff City made soccer history by beating Arsenal 1-0 in the FA Cup Final at Wembley in 1927, thus bringing the coveted trophy home to Wales.

The youngest member of that famous team was 19-year-old Ernie Curtis, who was the last surviving member of the side when we met at his Whitchurch home in 1989. Ernie had some marvellous tales to tell. Just imagine what it must have been like to be greeted by over 250,000 fans, many decked out in blue and white, as the team, holding the precious cup aloft, arrived back home in Cardiff. 'It was a welcome I will never forget, absolutely amazing', Ernie told me. These are just a couple of the highlights in a publishing career which provided scores of memorable occasions.

Perhaps one of the most pleasureable was being invited, as an old Windsor-Clive School pupil, to plant a tree with a time capsule at its base containing a copy of *Cardiff Yesterday*, as part of the school's 60th anniversary celebrations. How long it will remain underground is anybody's guess… in the meantime enjoy the nostalgic delights served up for us by Brian in his latest collection of oldies.

Stewart Williams (author/publisher of *Cardiff Yesterday*)

CHAPTER ONE
City Centre Scenes

This was the view from the roof of Snelling House, the Wales Gas Board headquarters in Bute Terrace, showing the neighbouring one-way street system and new car park, *c.*1970.

The young lady is passing the Taj Mahal Indian restaurant in Bridge Street which will be remembered by many Cardiffians, *c.*1960.

There was a sale on at C. Abraham & Sons the tailors in Bridge Street in 1964.

In this 1971 picture of Bridge Street, Gaba & Co. Ltd Wholesale Warehouse is on the right of the picture and F. Kiss the watchmaker's shop can be seen on the extreme left.

These Bridge Street properties were demolished to make way for a multi-storey car park. Note the Mill Lane entrance to Wyndham Arcade in the background, *c*.1967.

The John Bull Stores in Bridge Street had already been closed when this picture was taken in 1968.

The Bridge Street properties in this 1960s picture are long gone, but the Masonic Hall building which can be seen in the centre has survived.

The Co-operative Wholesale Society warehouse in Bute Terrace was built in 1891, but it looked in a sorry state when this picture was taken of it in 1936.

From the 1950s onwards, thousands of the inhabitants of these city centre dwellings, which were demolished, were moved to council estates on the outskirts of the city. This picture was taken in 1964.

The New Wales Gas Board headquarters in Churchill Way dwarfs their old offices, seen to the right of the building, c.1983. The chimney stack left of picture can be seen in the previous one.

Workmen levelling the banks of the Docks Feeder in preparation for the scheme to build a roadway over it reaching from Queen Street to Bute Terrace, 1947.

Concrete slabs, each weighing more than seven tons, were placed over the Docks Feeder between Pembroke Terrace and Edward Terrace in 1948.

The Docks Feeder now runs beneath the renamed Churchill Way. Guildford Crescent swimming baths, which closed in 1984, can be seen in the background.

Duke Street, formerly known as Shoemaker Street, was widened in 1924. The Duke Street Arcade which leads to High Street and St John Street was built in 1902. This picture was taken in the 1960s.

Another 1960s scene showing Castle Street. The ornate building where a van is parked outside is the Castle Arcade, built in 1887.

Church Street in 1980, showing St John's Church, which was built as a chapel of ease to St Mary's Church.

The busy junction of Church Street and Trinity Street, *c*.1988.

Caroline Street by night. It was dubbed 'Chip Alley' because of its many cafés and fish and chip shops.

The quaintly named Paradise Place which
was demolished in the 1980s. On the right of
picture can be seen the Taff Vale pub in
Queen Street.

The shops in this 1980
section of Queen Street
– Calders, Littlewoods,
Ratners and Mothercare
– are all gone today.

The Park Hotel in Park Place, right of picture, is now part of the Thistle Group.

St John Street is more popularly known as St John's Square. When this picture was taken the Owain Glyndwr to the right of St John's Church was known as the Buccanneer.

It is hard to believe that in the distant past the local pack of hounds would meet on what is now the corner of Charles Street and Queen Street.

Frederick Street was once known as Great Frederick Street. The warehouses to the left of the picture were to let when this picture was taken, but they have long been demolished.

Evan Roberts on the corner of Kingsway and Queen Street was demolished in 1985.

These premises on the corner of Dumfries Place and Queen Street were knocked down to make way for a multi-storey car park. Part of Queen Street Bridge can be seen to the right of this 1969 picture.

The Capitol Exchange Shopping Centre, opened in 1991, was built on the site of these Queen Street shops, seen here in1969.

Back in 1968, numbers 3, 4, 5 and 6 St Andrew's Place could have been bought for a total of £118,000!

The once grand Dumfries Place Drill Hall, the scene of many exhibitions, boxing and wrestling tournaments over the years, is now just a memory.

Magnet House, Kingsway, now the site of the splendid new building known as Number 1 Kingsway, in 1963.

This was Love Lane in 1949. It was another city centre street which disappeared when the area was redeveloped in the 1950s and '60s.

The residents of these empty houses in Rodney Street had all moved to pastures new when this picture was taken in 1965.

The Wesleylan Day School which stood in Working Street opposite the old Central Library. The Cardiff Masonic Hall is adjacent to it. The school, which was renowned for its skilled rugby players, closed in 1895.

Frederick Street looking towards Queen Street. The little terraced houses that had stood to the left of the picture had already been demolished when this picture was taken in 1967.
Inset: Mr Patrick Donovan, who lived at 59 Frederick Street, is seen here with his daughter Joanna, the author's mother. The Donovans brought up eight children (five boys and three girls) in this small two-bedroomed house.

This was the St Mary Street of 1971. It takes its name from St Mary's Church, which was badly damaged in the great flood of 1607. Extreme left can be seen part of the Great Western Hotel, built in 1876.

St Mary Street scene in 1960. The entrance to the Cardiff Market can be seen in the centre of the picture.

An important feature of ancient Cardiff was its town wall and gates. This wall running across the moat of Cardiff Castle was believed to be part of it. This photograph was taken in 1974.

High Street was once the principal street of the mediaeval borough. The entrance to High Street Arcade can be seen on the right of the picture.

Trolley bus wires were much in evidence when this picture of High Street was taken in 1962.

The old Custom House, built in 1845, is left of picture. On the extreme right is part of the Central Hotel which was destroyed in a fire in 2003.

Queen Street in November 1975. On the left is the Midland Bank, now HSBC, a single-storey building with Portland Stone pillars built in 1919.

The white building in the centre is the Wood Street Congregational Church, once known as the Temperance Town Music Hall. It was demolished in 1972.

Hundreds of shoppers queue outside James Howell & Co. for the summer sales of 1958.

This was Queen Street in 1975 before it was pedestrianised.

The corner block in Queen Street which was demolished to make way for the new shopping complex. Note the Christmas tree in the centre of the picture, which dates from 1982.

One of the street decorations for the St Mary Street Shopping Festival of 1964.

CHAPTER TWO
Shops and Businesses

Calder & Sons Mans Shop on the junction of Churchill Way and Queen Street, December 1967. Note the seasonal snow and Christmas decorations.

British Home Stores moved from their home of 30 years on the corner of Queen Street to bigger premises in the same street at the former Woolworth store in 1985. It was in 1955 that the store opened on the site of the old Carlton Restaurant.

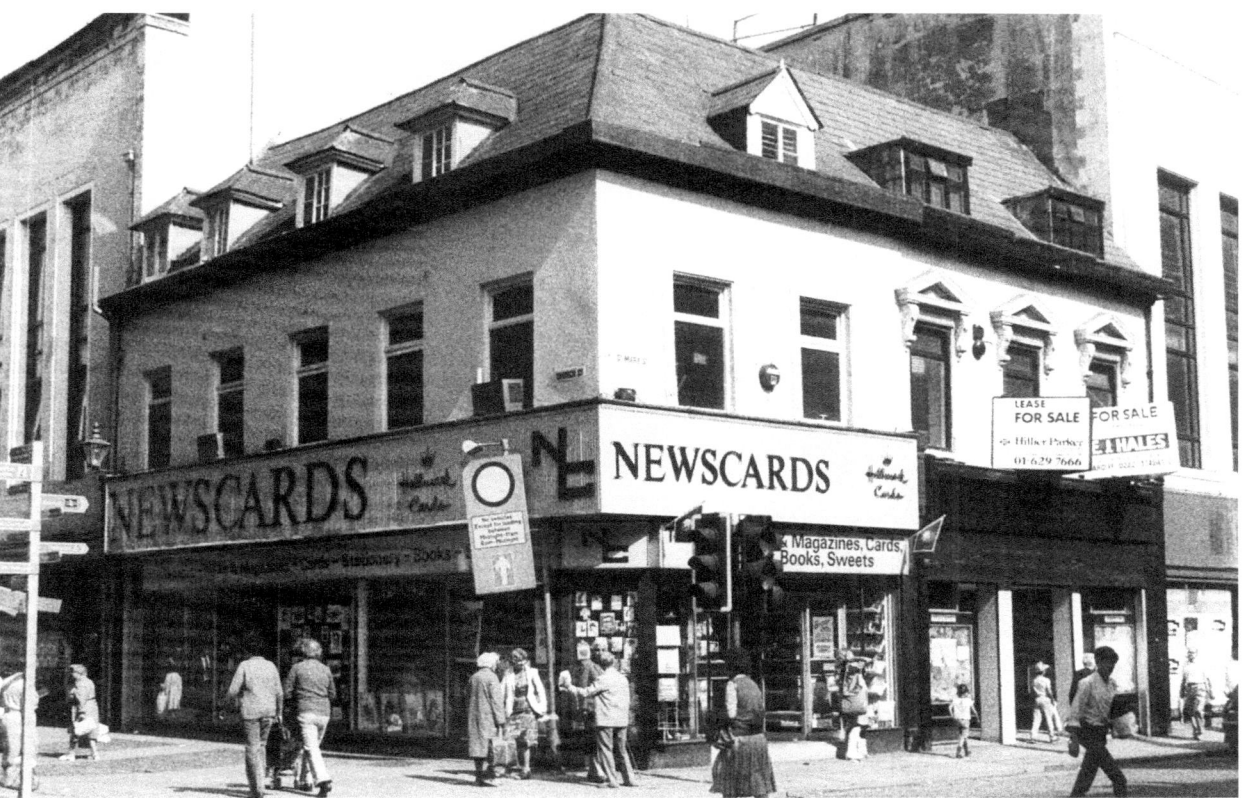

This early 18th-century listed building, on the corner of Church Street and St Mary Street, was originally known as the Corner House and was the town residence of Squire John Richards. The photograph was taken in 1987.

Olivers, on the corner of High Street and Church Street, seen here in 1977 commenced trading in Cardiff in 1918 and only ceased trading after many, many years.

The popular Mackross store in Queen Street, *c.*1975.

A blot on the landscape! All the shop fronts in this 1984 picture, apart from Greenfields, have retained the upper structure Victorian masonry.

Red Dragon (Travel) Ltd, Church Street, *c*.1968. The premises are now used as a restaurant.

Marments, Queen Street, traded in Cardiff from 1879 until 1986.

Hardy & Co was situated on the corner of Frederick Street and Queen Street and is seen here as it was in 1979.

The modern frontage of 2007 in Queen Street did not blend in with the rest of the building. The entrance to Andrews Arcade can be seen on the extreme right in this 1980 photograph.

With so many shoe shops in Queen Street there was certainly a need for Scholl foot comfort service in 1980.

Van Allan, Queen Street, was adjacent to the imposing Midland Bank building.

T.C. Palmer, Queen Street. To the left is the Taff Vale pub, which was demolished in 1978.

Ratners, 'Jewellers of Repute' in Queen Street, long before those infamous remarks were made!

John Menzies and Dunn & Co., Queen Street. Both buildings look as though they are in need of refurbishment, *c.*1980.

Youngs Dress Hire and Nationwide Building Society, Queen Street.

Willsons in Queen Street was sold for more than £2.5 million in one of the biggest property deals of its kind in the city in 1981.

Swears & Wells, yet another Queen Street shop of the 1980s.

Chelsea Girl, Queen
Street, *c.*1980.

Woodhouse, Queen Street. The entrance to the Top
Rank Suite is left of picture.

Burton, Queen Street. The entrance to the Dominion Arcade is right of picture.

Littlewoods was a familiar sight for Queen Street shoppers for more than 50 years. It closed in 1998.

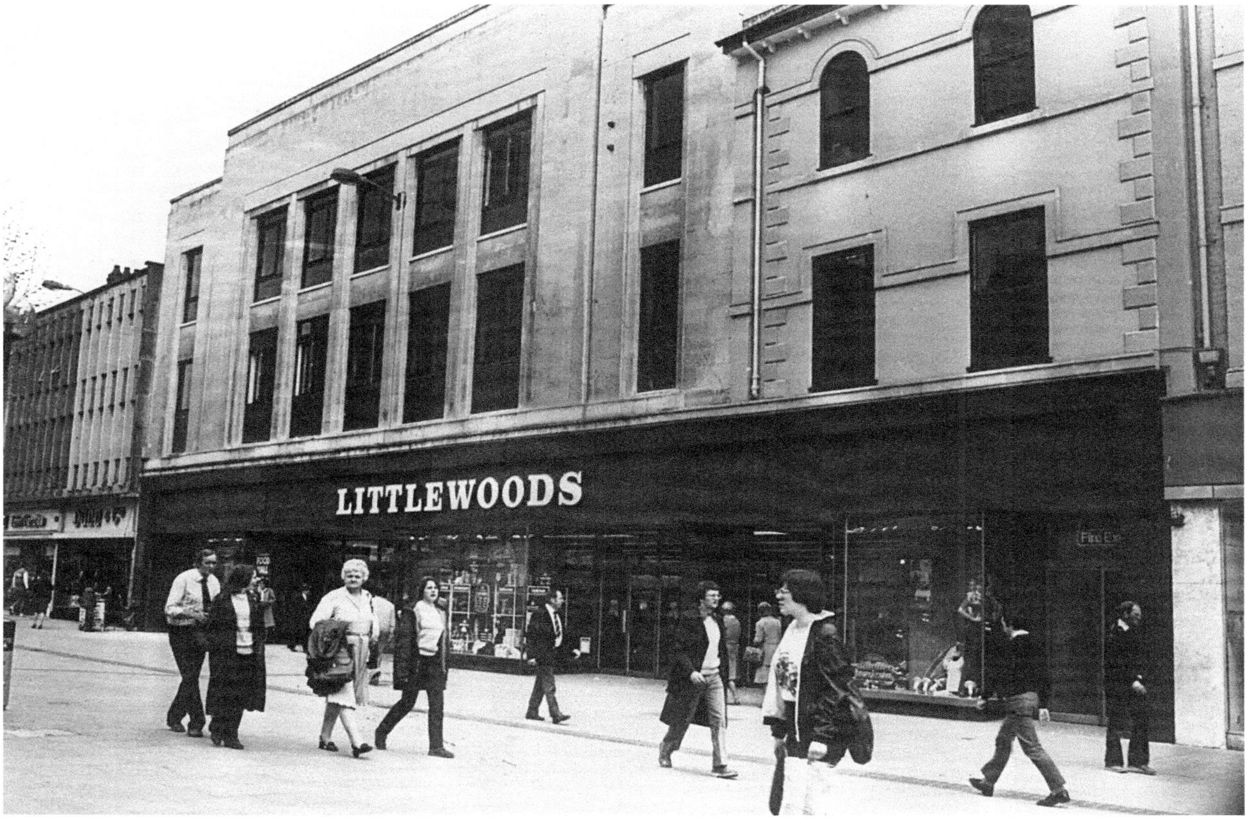

These Queen Street shops, numbers 109 to 119, were situated between the Park Hotel and Windsor Place and are seen here in 1981.

The old Dutch Café, Halfords and the Alexandra Hotel in Queen Street were demolished in the 1980s.

Evan Roberts was situated on the corner of Kingsway and Queen Street from 1922 until 1985 when the old building was demolished.

These two Queen Street shops, Dorothy Perkins and Loyds, were clearly in need of renovation in 1980.

It would have cost
just £3.95 to hire a
morning suit from
Dormie Dress Hire,
Queen Street, in the
1980s.

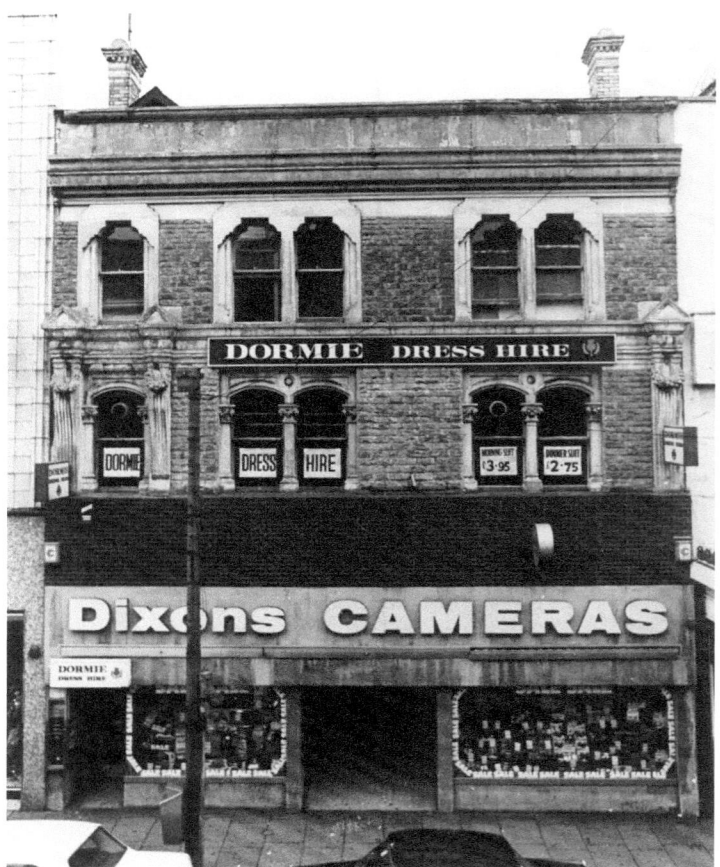

C & A Modes came to Queen
Street in 1963 and closed in
2003.

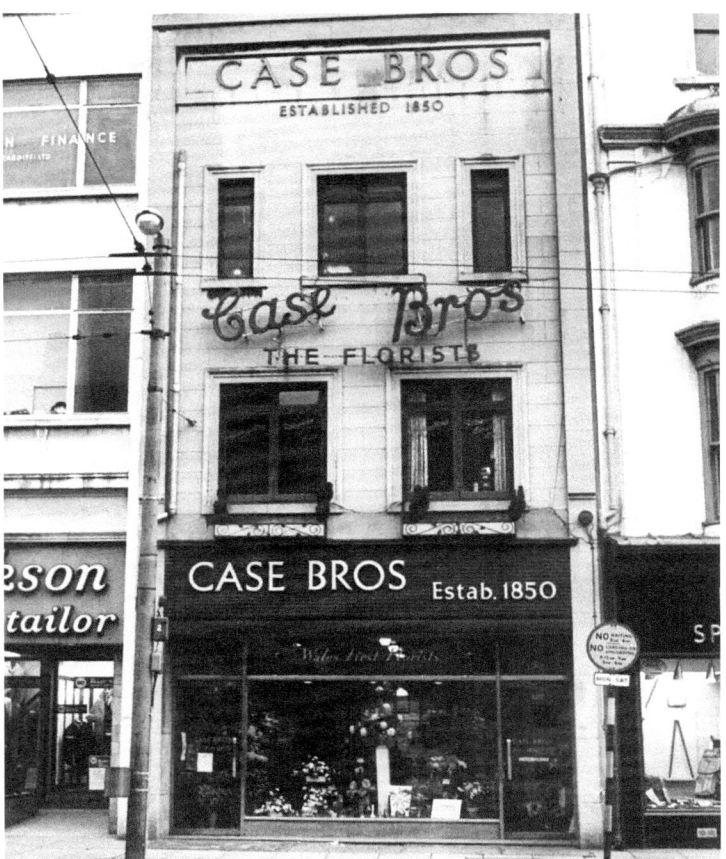

Case Bros, the old established florists in St John Street, 1966.

Cresta, the high-class gown shop in High Street.

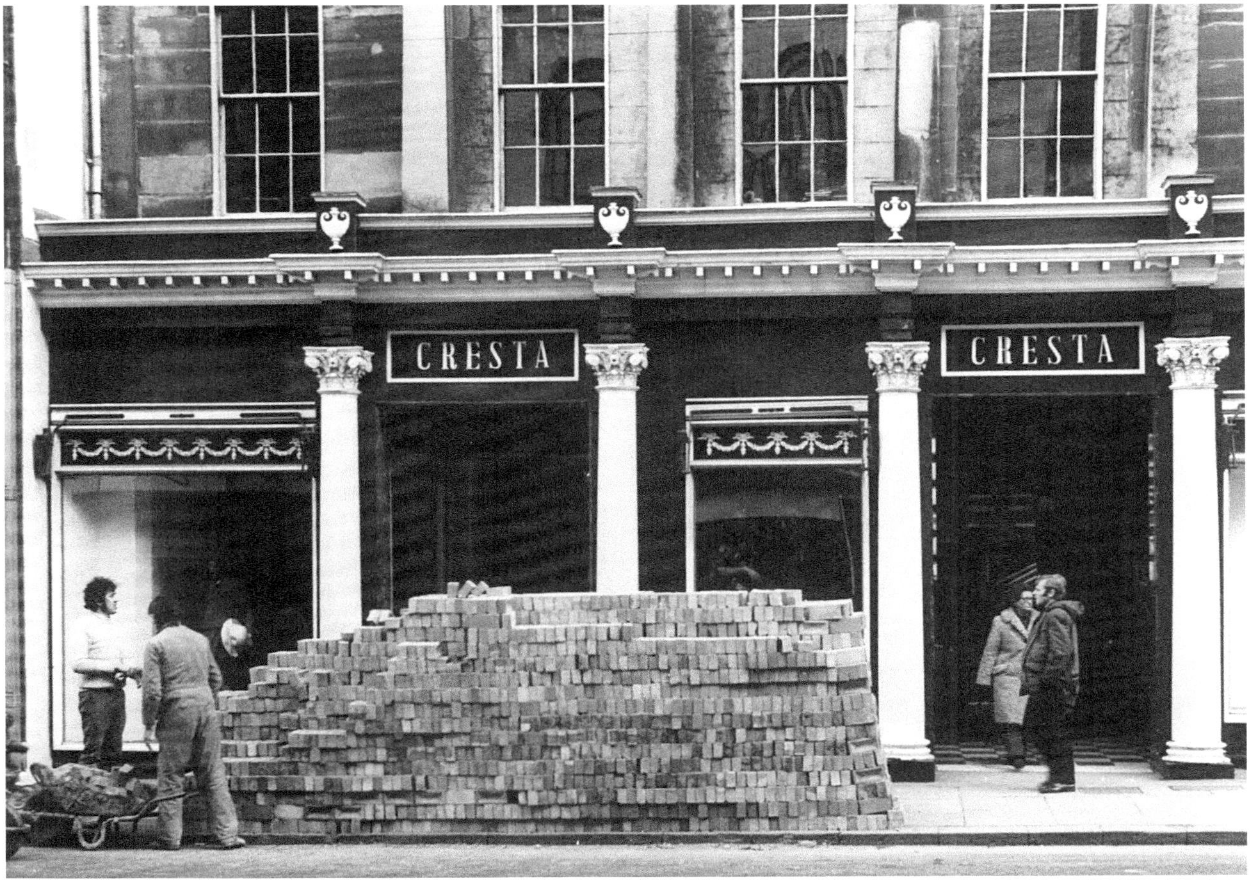

Victor Freed, Duke Street, 1964.

The Castle Street and Duke Street shops in this 1955 picture have all vanished from the scene.

CHAPTER THREE
Picture Palaces of the Past

The Empire, Capitol, Odeon, Olympia and Queens cinemas were all situated in Queen Street in 1955. Jane Wyman and Rock Hudson were starring in *All That Heaven Allows* at the Odeon and Van Johnson and Aldo Ray were starring in *Battle Cry* at the Olympia. A magnifying glass reveals that the classic western film *High Noon* was playing at the Queens cinema far right of picture.

The much loved Capitol cinema which had opened on Boxing Day 1921 was demolished in 1978.

The Odeon was originally known as the Imperial Picture Palace when it opened in 1911. Its most famous visitor was surely Hollywood actor Ronald Reagan, later to become the President of the United States of America. He visited Cardiff in 1949 to promote his film *The Voice of the Turtle*. The Cannon, right of picture, was previously known as the Olympia, ABC and later MGM.

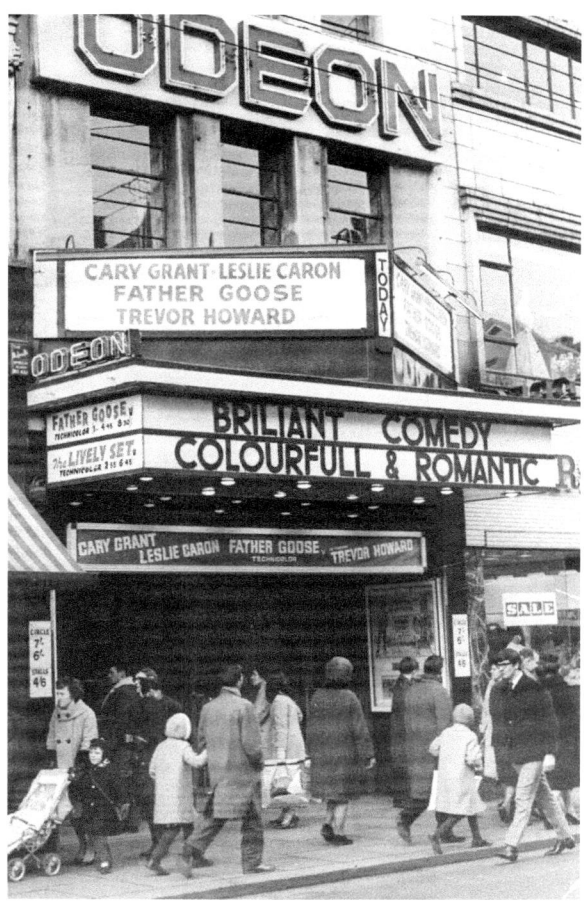

The 1964 comedy film *Father Goose* was playing at the Odeon. Note the spelling of the words Brilliant and Colourful!

Back in 1878, the Prince of Wales in St Mary Street was known as the Theatre Royal. Over the years, many famous thespians trod its boards. However, it became known for its sex films in the 1960s and closed as a cinema in 1984.

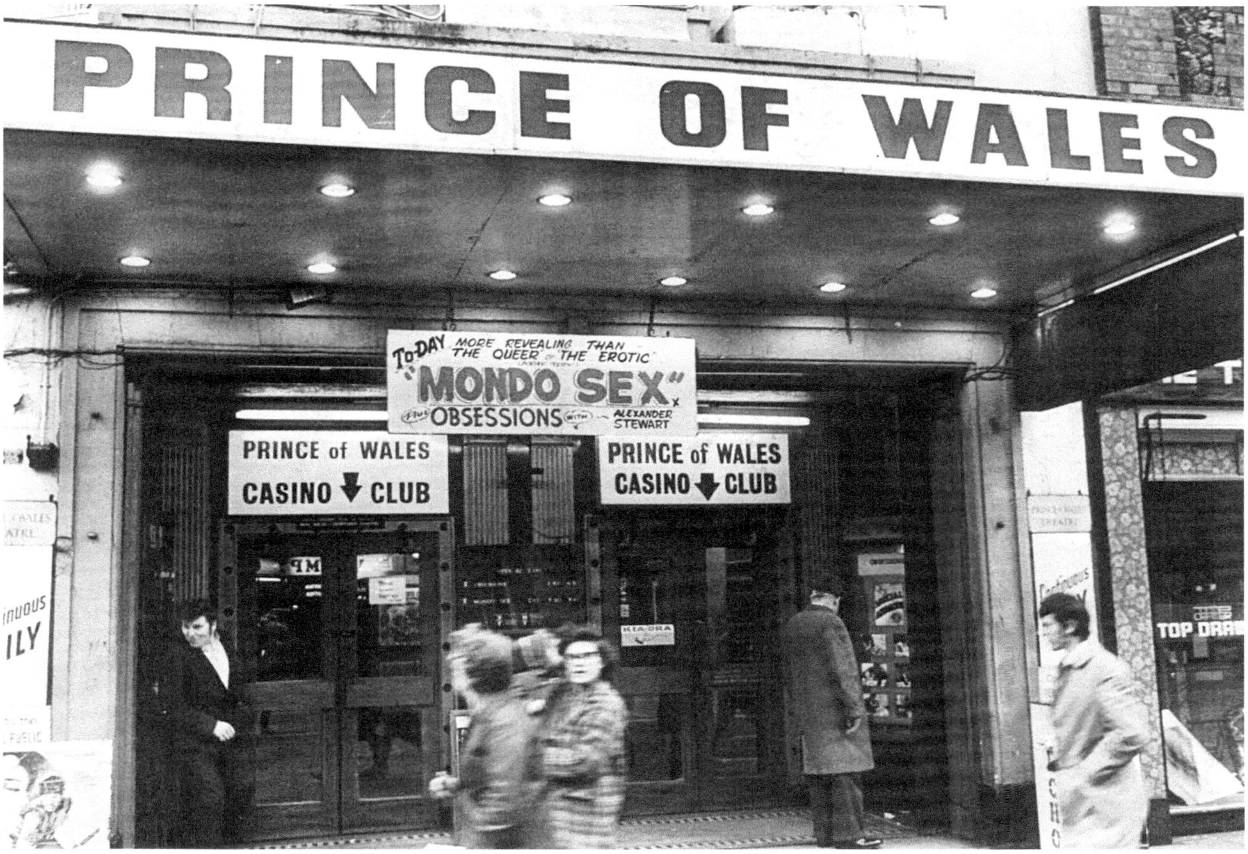

The Gala began life in 1889 as the Philharmonic Hall but most Cardiffians will remember this St Mary Street cinema as the Pavilion. It closed in 1968 and was later used as a bingo hall. (See p55, top picture.)

The Central Cinema on The Hayes was originally a roller skating rink. It was situated where Oxford House Arcade now stands. It opened in 1911 and closed in 1959.

The Gaumont Cinema closed in 1961 when the building was demolished to make way for C & A Mode. In 1887 it was known as Levino's Hall and two years later it became the Empire. It was known as the Gaumont from 1954.

The frontage of the Olympia in 1975 when Robert Redford was starring in *Three Days Of The Condor*.

The Queen's Cinema in Queen Street. In 1949 for the first time since the black-out was imposed in 1939 city streets were lit up with neon and other display signs.

This is how the Pavilion Cinema in St Mary Street looked in 1960 before it was converted to a bingo hall.

The Park Hall cinema in Park Place opened as a concert hall in 1885 and Winston Churchill once lectured there. This magnificent picture palace closed in 1971 and was demolished in 1980.

The King's Theatre in Westgate Street opened in 1887 as the Grand Theatre. It became the King's Theatre in 1904 and was later renamed the Hippodrome Palace.

Pictured outside the Plaza Cinema in Gabalfa in 1976 is Councillor Ian Jones, after his successful bid to stop the cinema being used for bingo. Unfortunately the cinema closed five years later and was demolished in 1985.

One of the last films to be shown at the Canton in Cowbridge Road East was *The Lost World* starring Michael Rennie and Jill St John. Once a popular silent picture house it closed in 1960.

The Coliseum in Canton closed in 1959 and was later a bingo hall.

The Ninian in Grangetown, which had seating for just 469 picture goers, closed in 1972 and was later used as a furniture store.

The Monico in Pantbach Road, Rhiwbina, was demolished in 2003. One of the city's oldest working cinemas, it had been showing films since 1937. Luxury apartments were being built on its site in 2003.

Popularly known as the 'Cora', the Coronet Cinema in Woodville Road was demolished in 1973 to make way for a garage. It closed in 1953 and the site is now occupied by a block of flats.

CHAPTER FOUR

Some Favourite Watering Holes

To the right of this 1960 picture can be seen the Royal Oak, Blue Anchor and the Terminus. The Royal Oak and Blue Anchor are no more and the Terminus is now Sam's Bar.

The demolition of the Griffin, sandwiched between the National Westminster Bank and the Trustee Savings Bank, in 1974, was described by Councillor Philip Dunleavy as 'public vandalism'.

The Globe Inn, which later became known as the Four Bars, in 1971.

Fulton Dunlop & Co. Ltd, St John Street, 1964.

The Alexandra Hotel on the corner of Station Terrace and Queen Street was up for sale in the 1960s.

The Taff Vale pub on the corner of Paradise Place and Queen Street was demolished in 1978.

The Marchioness of Bute, near the town end of Frederick Street, was demolished in the 1970s.

The Moulders Arms in Union Street was awaiting demolition in 1971.

The Salutation on the corner of Hayes Bridge Road and Homfray Street, which was demolished in 1982.

Regulars at the Salutation saying a special farewell before the bulldozers moved in to destroy their favourite pub.
Behind the bar are licensees Phyllis and Tony Blood proposing a toast.

The Hastings Hotel in Herbert Street in 1914. Mrs Beatrice Clode, standing in the doorway on the left with her two children, was the licensee at the time and remained there throughout World War One while her husband Sidney, a well-known Docks butcher, served in the army. The hotel was demolished in 1966 with the rest of the Newtown area.

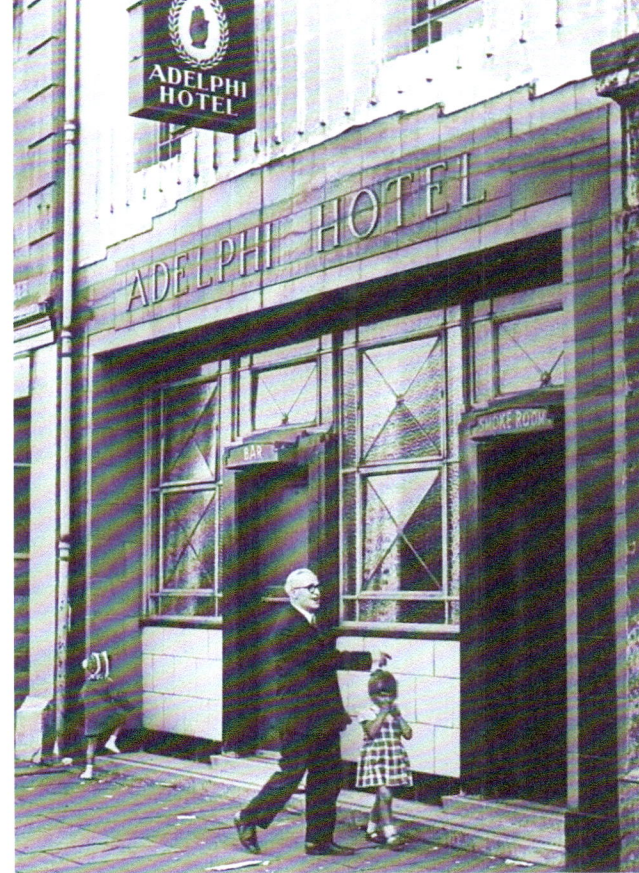

The Adelphi Hotel in Bute Street was due for demolition in 1961. Whatever happened to the two well-dressed little girls?

The first port of call for seamen and dockers used to be the Mount Stuart, just outside the Docks gates in Bute Crescent.

This is how the Canton Hotel looked in the 19th century when Colin Lewis Clarke was the licensee.

The Wyndham Hotel at the junction of Wellington Street and Cowbridge Road East is now being used as offices. It is seen here in 1971.

The Eagle Hotel, Davis Street, Adamsdown, was due for demolition in 1968.

The Driscoll family, who ran the pub for 40 years, posed for this picture outside the Bridgwater Arms, which was demolished in the late 1940s to make space for Churchill Way.

CHAPTER FIVE
Transport

Horse-drawn trams were still in evidence in Cardiff around 1900. The driver of this horse-drawn coach was Thomas George Jones. Travellers staying at the Queen's Hotel were collected at the railway station and driven to the hotel.

Electric trams came to Cardiff on 1 May 1902. This one is seen travelling through Queen Street, but note the other modes of transport still in use.

The first trolleybuses, seen here in High Street, operated in Cardiff in 1942 and were a regular sight on the roads for the next 28 years.

A busy St Mary Street and a trolleybus is heading towards High Street, 1962.

This trolleybus in Newport Road was number 262 and it belonged to the Cardiff Trolleybus Society. It had been specially decorated with coloured lights and flags to signal the start of celebrations to mark the end of the trolleybus system in the city, January 1970.

These two trams had ample space to turn around at Roath Park in 1937.

Old Faithful, the last tramcar, passes along Whitchurch Road proudly bearing the dates 1902–1950. Now there is talk of trams returning to the city!

One of the 32 Daimler Fleet Line buses bought for a total cost of £256,767 in 1967 by Cardiff City Transport.

A new fleet of minibuses operated in the city in 1988. Cardiff bus training officer, Mr Tony Hardy, with one of the new drivers, Mr Richard Brain, is in the front, with the other 'Clipper' drivers in the background.

The old Taff Vale Railway Station building had more character about it than the present Queen Street Station which replaced it.

A crowded Queen Street Station after delays caused by a reduced train service, due to a rail go-slow, in May 1972.

The year is 1955 and for the first time in 50 years Cardiff taxi-drivers operating outside the General Station had to move their taxi-rank from the station approach to the space between the bar buffet and the corporation transport offices, far right. The move was brought about by a new traffic system outside the station.

One of the causes of major traffic jams in the Grangetown area in December 1979 was the flooded Clare Road Bridge.

In August 1961 traffic to and from Cardiff Docks had to make a detour when the high tide caused flooding under Bute Street Bridge.

On one day in August in 1977 more than six weeks' rain fell on Cardiff in just 24 hours. Obviously, the car stuck in the water under Salisbury Road Bridge did not belong to these two women, judging by the smiles on their faces.

CHAPTER SIX

When Cardiff Went to the Dogs

Greyhound racing first came to Wales on 7 April 1928 at the Welsh White City Stadium at Sloper Road, Cardiff. It was so popular that shortly afterwards two meetings a week were also being held at the famous Cardiff Arms Park. This picture was taken in 1966.

These dogs were competing in the BBC Sportsview Television Trophy. Note the packed stands, c.1964.

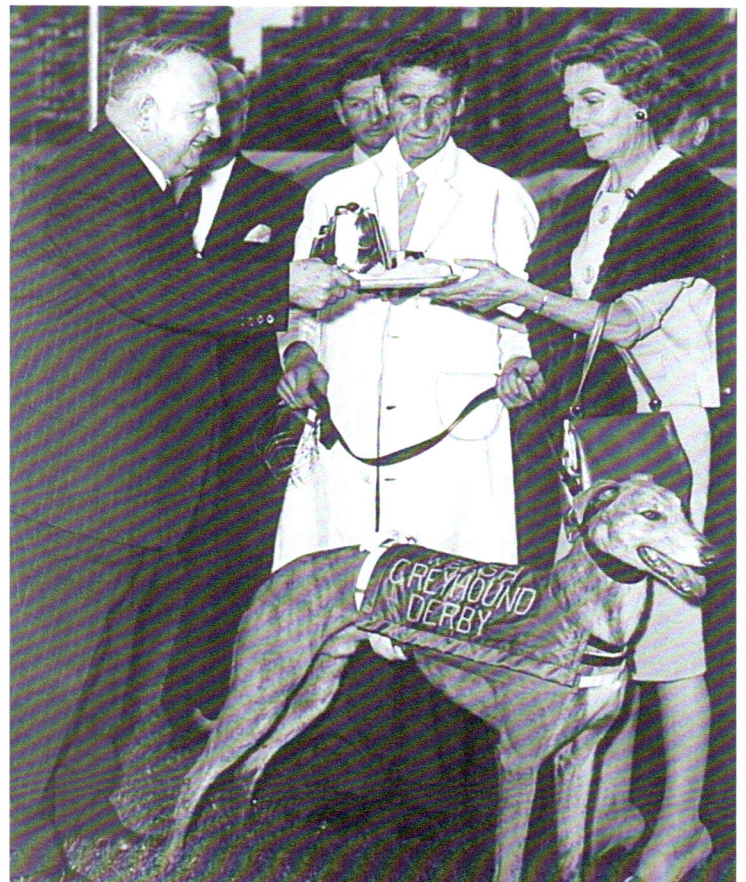

The Welsh Greyhound Derby was held at the Welsh White City Stadium between 1928–38 before being staged at the Cardiff Arms Park between 1945 and 1977 when the track closed. This picture shows the 1963 winner Fairy's Chum, who clocked the good time of 29.49 for 525 yards.

In 1930, the legendary Mick the Miller, the most famous dog in greyhound racing history, broke the world record for the standard distance of 525 yards on two occasions when competing in the Welsh Greyhound Derby at the Welsh White City Stadium.

Tom Cronin, who worked as a kennel man at the Cefn Mably kennels at St Mellons, Cardiff, is seen here with local top grade greyhound Harrow Bridge, *c.*1965.

Dickie Kelly, trainer, (standing) and some of his kennel men at Cefn Mably Kennels.

One well-known trainer was Bill Doolan, who started his training career at the old Sloper Road stadium. His favourite memory was of meeting Hollywood film star Rita Hayworth after his dog Fiery Fred had won the Rita Hayworth Stakes at one of the London tracks.

CHAPTER SEVEN
Cardiff at Work

Workmen laying new pipes on Rumney Hill in October 1967.

These workmen are levelling off the former wholesale fruit market island between Custom House Street and New Street in preparation for use as a temporary car park. The Lord Bute monument is in the background in 1966.

Another bit of Cardiff history bit the dust in 1975 when the Golate between St Mary Street and Westgate Street was transformed from a quiet lane to an access road for a new office block. The Golate dates from the Middle Ages when the River Taff flowed along what is now Westgate Street.

In this picture of the Golate, looking towards St Mary Street, the old *Western Mail & Echo* building, which had stood right of picture, had been demolished. The gentleman wearing a hat is the author's father, Billy Lee, who worked on the *South Wales Echo* for more than 50 years.

This was the scene in Custom House Street one day in May 1961. The little boy wearing wellies is collecting broken boxes for firewood.

Mrs Jane Buckley (left) and Mrs Jayne
Harvey, who both ran shops in Queen
Street, look on in 1986 as Wales Gas
workers reopen a hole in the ground that
was refilled following work by the South
Wales Electricity Board a fortnight
earlier.

Cardiff Dock workers waiting outside
Transport House in Charles Street before
attending a meeting in 1967.

Picketing the Western Area pumping station in Penarth Road in 1970 were, left to right, Mr William Power, of Ely, Mr Robert Swift, of Grangetown, and Mr William Barron of Canton. The pumping station is now an antique centre.

Pictured are the staff of the Maypole in High Street, which opened on 8 December 1888.

A.D. Davis, Canton Fish Market, in Cowbridge Road East.

David Harding ran a cycle shop in Cowbridge Road East for many years. The picture dates from 1960.

The staff of Peacocks store in the town centre, 10 May 1933.

Howell's drivers outside the company's garage in Charles Street.

In 1981, a seascape mural on the side of the Union of Shop Distributive and Allied Workers Union headquarters was unveiled. From left to right are Mr Steven Spode, Prince of Wales Committee, Mr Arthur Gilbert, general manager Marks and Spencer, Mrs Maureen Jones, store secretary, Marks and Spencer, Mrs Pat Phillips, deputy divisional officer USDAW, artists Mr Adrian Butler and Louise Shenstone who painted the mural, and Father Bernard Whitehouse, administrator of St David's Cathedral, Charles Street.

Mrs Caroline Royale, the Household Department manageress of Littlewoods, checking goods in the newly-opened extension with assistant Miss Lesley Bennett. The store closed in 1998.

Manager and staff of the Globe cinema in Albany Road. Left to right are Mrs Emily Hopkins, Mrs Lila Danter (usherettes), Mrs Ingrid Wardle (wife of the manager and acting cashier), Mr Ken Wardle (manager), Miss Phyllis Bevan (usherette) and Mr Keith Siddal (projectionist).

A woman's work is never done! Mrs Alice Huntley of 51 Wimborne Street, Splott, cleans the outside of her house watched by her granddaughter Ann, aged eight years, in 1972.

Mrs Hannah Court is pictured cleaning the back window of her home in Portmanmoor Road in September 1956.

With the old East Moors steelworks in the background, Mr Jim Mapstone and his three-year-old daughter Tammy enjoy the newly reclaimed area of parkland, 1978.

The East Moors steelworks, which ceased to exist as a production unit on 28 April 1978.

British Steel Corporation workers feeding the furnaces. Steel was first made in Cardiff in 1891.

The last steel made at East Moors flowed from B Furnace on 28 April 1978.

Joe Evans from Rhiwbina, who worked at the East Moors steelworks all his working life.

'Time for a cuppa'. A steelworker pours himself a mug of tea.

British Steel Corporation workers with their long service certificates, April 1978.

Steelworkers putting on a brave smile before the closure of the plant.

East Moors Steelworks engineer Jeff Thomas (right) presents Archie May, personal assistant to the chief engineer, with a silver coffee service on his retirement after 48 years loyal service.

Standing on the steps in front of the Tivoli Cinema, Station Road, Llandaff, is manager Mr Harris with his staff. The lady in the back row left of picture is Mrs Barbara Morgan. The cinema closed in 1959.

Standing on the roof of the Evan Roberts building in June 1977 are staff members Georgina Simpson, Lynne Thompson, Mary Auelis, Eric Down, Doris Dyer and Rita Johnson.

CHAPTER EIGHT
Lost Landmarks

The *Western Mail & Echo* offices which stood on the corner of St Mary Street and the Golate, *c*.1950.

The Taff Vale Railway Office and its well-known clock tower on the corner of Queen Street and Station Terrace. Built in 1860, it was demolished in 1973 and a block of luxury flats is now situated on the site.

This was Havelock Street, Temperance Town, in the 1920s.

Wood Street, which connected the lower part of St Mary Street and Tudor Road. The area was once owned by Colonel Wood and is seen here in 1920.

Bowcotts the butchers was situated on the corner of Wharton Street and Trinity Street. It was demolished in 1959 to make way for the new four-storey extension to James Howell's store.

Some older Cardiffians will still remember Lewis the tobacconist on the corner of High Street and Castle Street, 1957.

To the left of this picture taken in 1956 can be seen T.P. Martin, Chemist, in Castle Street, which closed 10 years later in 1966.

One of the oldest streets in Canton is Delta Street. The building on the right used to be a saddlers and before that a blacksmith. The poster informs us that Waldini's popular gipsy band was playing at the Park Hall theatre.

St David's Hospital, Canton. It opened as the Union Workhouse in 1836 and later became the City Lodge. The site has been redeveloped, but the façade of the building was retained.

The Salvation Army
Men's Hostel in Bute
Street, 1968. It was
demolished and a new
hostel was opened in
1976.

A landmark for
thousands of people was
the Cory Hall in Station
Terrace, which was
demolished in 1985.

The Odeon and ABC cinemas in a pedestrianised Queen Street, 1981.

Alexandre, the gentlemen's outfitters left of picture, is now a Sainsbury's supermarket. When this picture was taken in 1978, the multi-storey car park had yet to be built.

There cannot have been many Cardiffians over the years who never gazed in the window of Arthur Kaltenbach the jeweller and watchmaker in Caroline Street, seen here in 1983.

Rotosky the Kosher butcher shop in Bridge Street, 1980. The Crown & Anchor pub is to the right of the café sign.

This was the scene from Rumney Hill in 1968. The power station to the right of the picture, like most of the other buildings in the background, is long gone.

A bird's-eye view of Cardiff Prison. In the background, to the right of the picture, can be seen the new Cardiff City Fire Station, which opened in 1973.

This 1963 picture of the Chain Library on the corner of Albany Road and Alfred Street should revive some half-forgotten memories of the area.

A well-known City Road landmark was the Gaiety Cinema, which opened in 1912 and closed in 1961. It was later used as a bingo hall.

Mr Gill Thomas, a carpenter employed by British Transport, makes one of his last trips through the subway before his retirement in 1963. The 400-yard long Ely Tubular Subway from Ferry Road to Penarth Docks, which went under the River Ely, opened to the public on 14 May 1900 and closed on 30 September 1963 when both entrances were bricked up. It cost £26,000 to build and pedestrians were charged a penny when it first opened, but entrance was free from 1937.

CHAPTER NINE

Cardiff at War

DIG FOR VICTORY... One of the most famous home front slogans of the World War Two was aimed at encouraging everyone to help grow food for the nation.

Preparing for war. Unloading ARP shelters at Newport Road sidings in April 1939.

Decontaminator squad, training at the quayside, east side at Bute East Dock, in 1944.

The Prime Minister, Winston Churchill, with the Lord Mayor of Cardiff outside the City Hall, 1941.

Four people and a dog were rescued from a Morrison shelter, seen in the foreground, when these houses in Penylan Road were wrecked after an air raid.

A man walks disconsolately up the path of what is left of his house in Prospect Drive, Fairwater.

A cleaning up operation after another air raid, this time in Partridge Road.

A deserted De Burgh Street, Riverside. Children used the bombed patches as playgrounds.

Neville Street, Canton, after an air raid in January 1941. Can you spot the two firemen?

These two houses in Glamorgan Street, Canton, were wrecked by a lone bomber four hours after the main raid. An Anderson air-raid shelter saved the occupants.

Firemen at East Moors Police Station with hoses and standpipe. Leading fireman Idris Jenkins is in the centre back row.

Five gallant Cardiff firemen whose heroism was recognised. Left to right: Sergeant D.J. Collins (Cardiff Fire Brigade), Sub-officer W. Brown (Cardiff Auxiliary Fire Service) and leading fireman N. Groom (Cardiff Auxiliary Fire Service) who were awarded the George Medal, and Sub-officer T. Fitzgerald (Cardiff Auxiliary Service) and Sergeant J.A. Germain (Cardiff Fire Brigade) who received commendations.

Sergeant H. Ginn, of Cardiff Police Force, outside Buckingham Palace after receiving the BEM.

Mrs Wakely, of School House, Llanishen Street, outside Buckingham Palace after receiving the MC awarded to her late son Lieutenant W. Wakely. She is seen with her husband, youngest son and late son's fiancée.

Spitfire pilot Flight Lieutenant George Andrew Martin, DFC, of Colchester Avenue. He destroyed 57 railway engines, 12 aircraft on the ground, two in the air and was hit at least 20 times when serving in Yugoslavia.

Christmas lunch was put on for these Welsh servicemen in the Drill Hall, 1945.

An avenue of trees was presented to the parishioners of Whitchurch by the Second Evacuation Hospital Unit of the United States Army in gratitude for hospitality during the war. The picture shows Mr Henry O. Ramsay, the American Consul in Cardiff, about to unveil a plaque on Whitchurch Common. Also in the picture are Mrs Ramsay, Councillor C.L. Tucker (chairman of the Whitchurch Parish Council) and Mrs Tucker.

These four Cardiff GI brides leaving for the USA are, left to right, Mrs E. Carvill, Mrs M. Ogden, Mrs B. McGregor and Mrs D. Fieldon.

GI bride Mrs Lucille Esch is being seen off by her brother and sister. She joined her husband who, following his demobilisation, was studying for the ministry at Fort Worth, Texas, 1946.

Setting off for a new life in Canada are these Cardiff women who all married Canadian solders during the war.

VE Day, Fairwater. One of the many bonfires that were lit throughout Cardiff by way of celebrating the end of the war. Usually, an effigy of Adolf Hitler was placed at the top of them.

The residents of Edward Street celebrate the end of the war with a street party. Edward Street was the last city centre street to be demolished when the area was redeveloped.

Grand Avenue, Ely. VE Day celebrations.

A policeman enjoys 'a cuppa' at the Snowdon Road VE Day party.

After the war celebrations at Caerwent Road.

The children have had their party, now its the turn of the adults of Baron Road.

The children of Oakley Road, Grangetown, enjoy their victory party.

VE Day party in Cathays. The children in these two pictures are from Miskin Street, Glynrhondda Street and Llanbleitian Gardens.

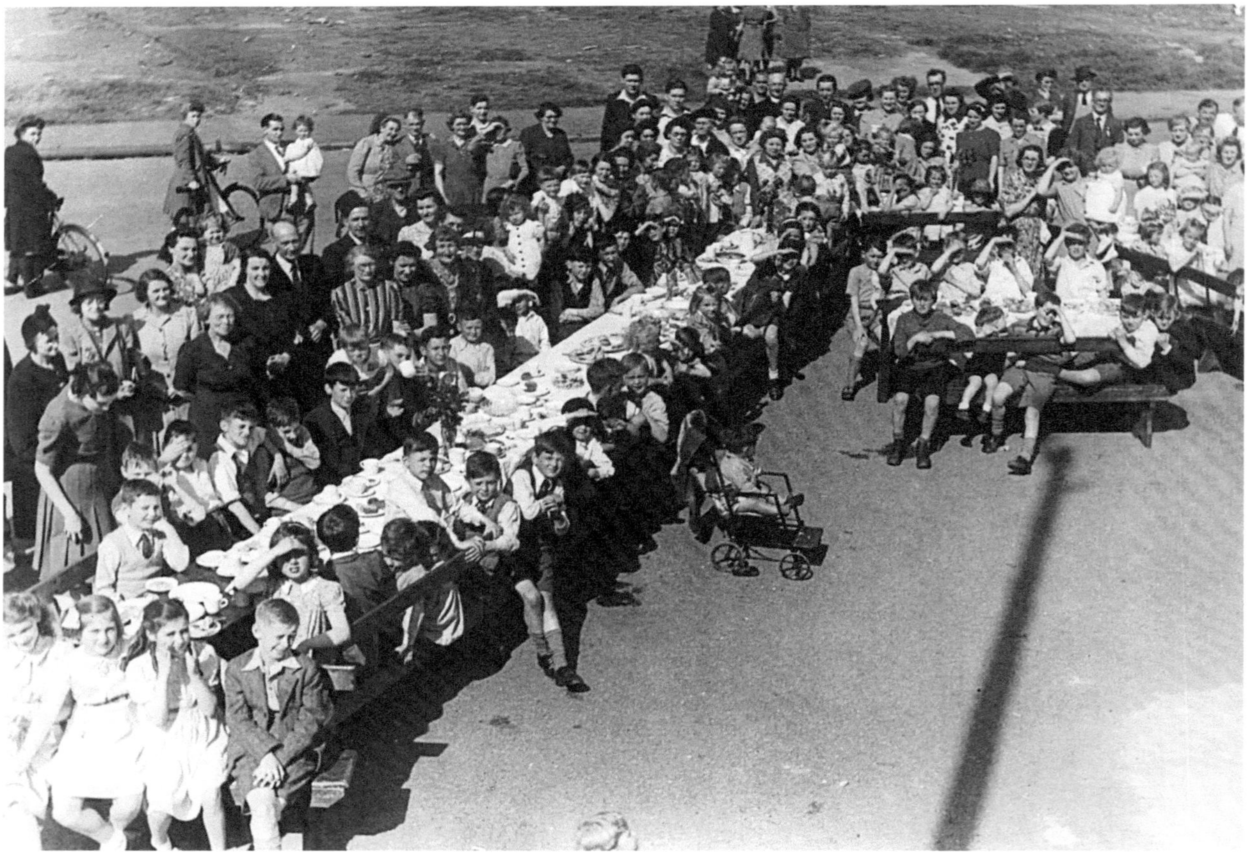

These Cardiff children celebrated the end of the hostilities with a fancy dress competition.

CHAPTER TEN
Law and Order

A crowd gathered outside Cardiff Prison to read the official death notice following the execution of a Canadian soldier, H.J. Grosseley, for the murder of a woman at Porthcawl, September 1945.

Cardiff Prison has seen a lot of changes since this picture was taken in 1957.

A familiar landmark on the corner of Cowbridge Road East and Market Road was the old Canton Police Station which dated to 1881. It had a bell tower to summon policemen and could easily have been mistaken for a castle. It was demolished in 1961.

Plenty of light, acres of glass, a pastel-coloured frontage. This is the building that replaced the old Canton Police Station, 1968.

Whitchurch Police Station at Bishop's Road was demolished in 2004.

At six foot and eight inches, PC Joe Young stood head and shoulders above his collegues. Dubbed 'Mighty Joe', the 17-stone copper is seen with his bodyguard Sabre in 1968.

A plaque to commemorate the police service to the city of Cardiff from 1836 until 1969 and the amalgamation of the Cardiff City force with the forces of Glamorgan, Swansea and Merthyr to form the South Wales Constabulary, was presented by the former chief constable of Cardiff Mr T.G. Morris, to the Lord Mayor of Cardiff. Mr Morris makes the presentation, watched by members of the merged force, Mrs Merrells, the Lady Mayoress, and Mrs Morris, 1971.

Old White Watch, Central Fire Station, March 1974.

The official opening
ceremony of the new Fire
Service Headquarters and
Central Fire Station in
Adam Street took place on
30 March 1973.

These firemen are seen in
the old Westgate Street
station, which was
demolished to make way
for a multi-storey car
park.

Firemen attending a fire in Miskin Street, Cathays, c.1970. The church in the centre has now been demolished.

CHAPTER ELEVEN
'Little Ireland' and the Docklands

After the Irish famine, hundreds of Irish families settled in houses built by the Third Marquis of Bute in an area of the town called Newtown or 'Little Ireland' as it was known to many Cardiffians. To the left can be seen the Crichton Arms in Tyndall Street.

This was Tyndall Street in 1964 when the news that the houses were going to be knocked down and the area used for industrial development was greeted with mixed reactions by the residents.

These children playing happily in Pendoylan Street were unaware that their homes would soon be due for demolition.

Three young men from Newtown, towels in hand, were probably going for a swim in Guildford Crescent Baths, *c*.1960.

The demolition of Newtown had already started in June 1967.

Mrs Patricia Rees and her two children were the only people remaining in Patrick Street, Butetown, in May 1969.

The famed Bute Street looking towards town, 1964.

Butetown in the 1950s. A. Salama's shop is behind the car on the corner of South Church Street.

Most of the properties in James Street had been bricked up in 1976. The Ship & Pilot, left of picture, was still serving pints though.

Mr Frederick Patterson (left), the James Street butcher, is seen with his assistant Thomas Nagle who had worked in the shop for 44 years in 1976.

The old and the new. The new multi-storey flats extend skywards in the background, 1964.

Ship Lane, Butetown, 1973.

One of the docks' most popular figures for more than 40 years was fishmonger Tommy Letton, who had a street named after him.

These residents of Crichton Street were served with compulsory purchase orders on their properties in 1975, but they didn't want to move. Left to right are Miss Sonja Jensen, Miss Maria Loizou, Mrs Elen Cotomanis, Mrs Sarah Jenkins and Mrs Dorothy Fahr. In the front are Mrs Phyllis Jensen and her granddaughter Anne.

The old and new Butetown exist side by side, 1970.

Councillor Philip Dunleavy looks at a pre-war Brains advert still surviving on a wall in one of the streets of Butetown, 1974.

Mrs Jeane Christian, aged 87, was one of the first tenants to move into the new block of flats in Loudoun Square in 1964. With her are Carolyn Merrifield of Burgess Partnership and Peter Jones, senior housing officer, Cardiff City Council.

An official of the National Docks Labour Board works from the call stand 'calling on men' for jobs in 1965. Each man's name went on to a roster and he was allocated a job as his name came up. The system originated in South Wales as the fairest method of giving out work. It was said to eliminate favouritism where 'plum' jobs were concerned.

Workers ripping up railway lines on a site for a new timber berth at Roath Dock, *c.*1965.

Dock workers unloading Canadian timber, Roath Dock. The ship to the right of the picture is the *George E. Embiricos, c.*1965.

The Bristol Channel Ship Repairers Dry Dock, 1976.

A cup of tea makes a welcome break for these men who have been unloading produce in and around the Custom House Street area since first light, 1960.

CHAPTER TWELVE

Memorable Moments

The Earl of Dumfries, who was celebrating his 13th birthday, declared Roath Park open for the use of the public on 20 June 1894.

Thousands of Cardiffians assembled at the civic centre on the occasion of the Coronation visit of King George VI and Queen Elizabeth on 1 July 1937.

The Lord Mayor of Cardiff, Alderman R.G. Robinson, officially opened Churchill Way after the Bute Docks Feeder had been covered over.

In 1947, the Marquess of Bute handed over Cardiff Castle and grounds to the people of Cardiff. This section of the crowd saw the ceremony outside the castle.

A section of the crowd waiting for the Churchill Way opening civic procession. The gentleman directly behind the lady wearing a brooch is William Bryant, who lived in Dalton Street, Cathays, and who later became the author's father-in-law.

Members of Rumney Conservative party, who did not want the County Cinema turned into a bingo hall, staged a demonstration in May 1977.

Mine hosts Tony Blood and his wife Phyllis at a charity function at the Salutation pub, where they manned the pumps for more than 25 years.

Fred Dark, chief general manager of the South Wales Division of the National Bus Company, presents Patricia Moore, Glamorgan County Archivist, with a painting of the first bus to operate between Cardiff and Penarth. On the left is Stewart Williams, author/publisher of the *Cardiff Yesterday* series of books, who at the time was publicity officer of Western Welsh Omnibus Company, April 1975.

The official reopening of the Market Tavern in Trinity Street in August 1983. Pictured are former dray-horse driver Sid Tudor (left) and Aubrey Jones, managing director of Welsh Brewers.

Were you one of them? Screaming Beatles fans outside the Capitol, *c.*1964.

The South Glamorgan Youth Brass Band give a short recital at the official opening of the Bandstand in Queen Street at the junction of Churchill Way, September 1984.

Councillor Paddy Kitson, chairman of South Glamorgan County Council, cuts the tape to mark the official opening of Schooner Way. Left to right are Councillor Ken Hutchings, chairman of highways, Councillor Paddy Kitson, Mrs Susan Williams, Lord Lieutenant of South Glamorgan, with her dog Snippet and Terry Latham, managing director of Tarmac Homes Bristol and West, 1988.

Attending a rehearsal for the *South Wales Echo* Fashion Spectacular at the sports hall of the University Hospital of Wales were choreographer Peter Benfield, Gillian Silver, Samantha Bennett, Margaret Lewis, Alison Thomas, Russell Knight, Jeanette Byrne, Shaan O'Carroll, Laura May and Julie Grant, 1983.

The Lord Mayor of Cardiff, Councillor John Iorweth Jones, helps to plant a plane tree in Queen Street to commemorate the Queen's Silver Jubilee, 1977.

The Lord Mayor's Parade, sadly now discontinued, used to attract thousands. The Midland Bank's Summer Time Special float turns into High Street, 1989.

Leading the Lord Mayor's Parade is the South Wales Constabulary Police Band, 1982.

The float of the 3rd (V) Battalion of the Royal Regiment of Wales, who were the winners of the 1st Military Class of the Lord Mayor's Parade, 1983.

Cardiff Shopping Festival Queen Gail Hassan with some of the girls on the Chamber of Trade float, August 1978.

Make Someone Buzz! Busby the British Telecom mascot is given a kiss after the British Telecom float won the Cardiff Chamber of Commerce Trophy at the Lord Mayor's Parade, 1983.

There were more than 60 floats in the Lord Mayor's Parade of 1984. And showing a shapely leg on the South Wales Police float were Debbie John (left) and Debbie Dutfield, both of Rumney Police Station.

Stephen Blackie, aged 10, leads members of the Butetown Youth Centre in song before the start of the 1978 Lord Mayor's Parade.

Cardiff Morris dancers in Church Street raising funds for the St John's Church tower, which can be seen in the background, 1976.

These two young men will never forget the time they sailed down Cowbridge Road East, Canton, in the flood of 1979.

Peter Bishop (left), seen here with driver Fred Jones, became the new transport manager of David Morgan Ltd in 1988. The much loved David Morgan store on The Hayes celebrated its centenary in 1979. Sadly, it is due be closed at the end of 2004 when the building will be demolished to make way for a new shopping complex.

A charity pancake race in aid of the RNLI was staged by staff of David Morgan Ltd in 1988.

Louise of David Morgan Ltd is off to a 'frying' start in the 1988 charity pancake race.

Carol Kinsey (first left seated), joint managing director of David Morgan Ltd, with some of the Morgan 'glamour girls', 1988.

John Morgan (left) with Mr Stuart Bailey holding a plaque which reads, 'David Morgan Ltd were pleased to be able to present the curtains in this room to the …Wales Railway Centre February 1988.'

John Morgan (left) of David Morgan Ltd presents Mr and Mrs Charles and Cora Welsby with a picture they won in the Cardiff In Bloom competition, 1990.

Cardiff became a city in 1905 and the first meeting of the city council took place on 23 October 1905.

This was the scene outside the City Hall in 1955, when Cardiff was proclaimed the capital city of Wales.

CHAPTER THIRTEEN
Happiest Days of Their Lives!

Stephen Powell (left) of Smith Street and Eric Horne of Robinson Square amid the broken walls and towering steelworks. They and their families were about to be rehoused in Tremorfa, 1970.

'Come On The Bluebirds'. Young supporters at Cardiff City's Ninian Park, 1969.

These pupils of Adamsdown Primary School had to wash their hands in cold water in the school playground cloakroom, *c.*1974.

Children at the Rainbow Club gather round to watch five-year-old Roheim Bux light the candle in the 'Lights of Friendship' ceremony, part of the children's United Nations Day Celebrations at a party given to the children by George Davey, 1961.

James Howell's
children's Christmas
party, *c*.1950.

Pupils of Cathays
National School in
Little Wyeverne Road,
which was known to
many as Jerry's College.
It was demolished
sometime after World
War Two.

Girl pupils of St Peter's Secondary Modern School, St Peter Street. A block of flats now stands where the school was situated. This picture dates from 1949.

These girls from Gladstone School, Whitchurch Road, posed for this picture outside the National Museum of Wales in 1954.

The Lady Margaret High School for Girls was situated off Colchester Avenue. This picture of form 2C was taken in 1954.

Our Lady's Convent, like Lady Margaret School, no longer exists. These girls were photographed in 1949.

Our Lady's Convent, *c.*1947.

Christmas Party at Peter Lea School, Fairwater, 1957. The girl second from right is Christine Donovan. Others in the picture are Robert Tucker, Susan Hill and Rita Silver.

Second and third prize winners in the ideas section, age six to 11, of the Civic Awards Scheme, were Glyncoed Junior School, Pentwyn, and Mountstuart Primary School. Pictured are the Glyncoed youngsters (front) left to right: Rachel Stephenson, Dawn Craig, Emma Davies, Clare Fox, Matthew Roberts and Stephen Davey, with their £50 cheque, won for a suggestion to improve a park at Waun Fach, Pentwyn. Behind, left to right: Mountstuart pupils John Gerrish, Mathew Percy, Zoltan Miller, Stuart Rutledge, Nadia Pearce, Raymond Hassan, Julian Konten and Gavin Neizer, who won £25 when they suggested a quiet garden area for pensioners inside the school grounds, 1984.

Youngsters from the Maureen Rego School of Dancing get ready for the Lord Mayor's Parade of 1983.

Llanrumney High School football team, 1965.

Llanrumney High School baseball team. John Smith (centre) went on to captain Wales a record number of times.

The Cardiff Schools junior baseball team, July 1964.

One of the many paper boys who delivered the *Echo* to hundreds of houses in the Cardiff area in the 1970s was Russell Harvey of Cyncoed.

The Two Penny Rush! Childrens' cinema matinée performances were very popular between the 1930s and 1950s. These children are seen rushing out of the Capitol Cinema, 1937.

CHAPTER FOURTEEN
Leisure and Pleasure

The Ocean Club, Tremorfa, was a popular venue for dances in the 1960s.

The interior of the Ocean Club. On the right is the bar and on the left the dance floor.

The Sophia Gardens Pavilion was built for the 1951 Festival of Britain. Business exhibitions, dances, boxing, wrestling and various other events were staged there until the roof caved in after a heavy snowstorm in 1982.

Alyson Jones, aged 14, of Penylan, laces up her skates before joining in the roller skating at the Sophia Gardens Pavilion, 1982.

This was the entrance to
the Club Roma in
Churchill Way, 1967.

One of the big attractions for members of the
Casino Club in Bute Road was the game of
'blackjack', 1965.

'Let's Go To The Hop'. Teenagers dancing at the Top Rank Suite in Queen Street, November 1965.

East Moors steelworkers pensioners' outing, 1980.

'Smile please'. East Moors retired steelworkers' outing, c.1978.

These workers and their wives are enjoying a drink or two in the East Moors Steelworkers Sports and Social Club in Sloper Road, c.1977.

'We won the cup'. Bobby Rees (left), was captain of the Vulgan pub team which won the Cardiff league darts championship, *c*.1970.

Winners of the Cardiff league and pairs darts competition show off their trophies at the Newbridge Inn, Trowbridge, *c*.1977.

Some Cardiffians will remember 'The Castaways' bar in the Buccaneer, now the Owain Glyndwr. The décor included trees, a sunny tropical view with moving clouds and the sound of the sea and seagulls, 1966.

Saturday nights in the Sandringham Hotel in the 1960s were great fun. The picture dates from 1962.

One of the main venues for weddings in the 1970s was the Central Hotel at the top end of St Mary Street. It was ravaged by fire for the second time in its 120-year history on 2 January 2003.

Another hotel which is just a memory is the Bristol Hotel, which used to be in Penarth Road. Patrons used to enjoy live bands and discos there twice a week. It is seen here in 1968.

The Queen's Hotel in St Mary Street, which closed in 1974.

The Royal Hotel in St Mary Street has changed a lot since this picture was taken in 1962. It underwent a multi-million pound refurbishment in 2001.

The Old Arcade, Church Street. Left to right are George Hoskins, Bernard 'Slogger' Templeman, landlord Vernon Barber, Terry Flynn and John Hoskins with pictures of their late friend, Cardiff boxer Joe Erskine, c.1990.

John Rees, landlord of the Ruperra Arms in Ordell Street, is pictured outside his pub, which was a great favourite with the East Moors steelworkers.

Office workers and
other patrons of
the Packet Hotel in
James Street
enjoying a
lunchtime pint,
1988.

The Merchant Navy Hotel,
which later became the
Station Hotel. The General
Railway Station is extreme left
of the picture, which was
taken in 1988.

In the centre is the Llanishen Indoor Bowling Stadium in Rhyd-y-Penau Road.

How it looked after the roof collapsed during a heavy snowstorm in January 1982. Mr Richard Lewis (left) of the stadium and Mr Alen Pasley, of E. Turner & Sons, survey the damage.

The interior of the Llanishen Indoor Bowling Stadium. It later became the Bowls Social Club, but was demolished in 2004 to make way for a block of luxury flats.

A consortium of bowlers took over the stadium in 1973 and this picture shows Welsh international bowler Mr W.J. 'Billy' Mills, the managing director of the new company with fellow director Mr Tudor Williams.

Management and staff of the Llanishen Leisure Centre. Fourteen-year-old Carolyn Williams, of Whitchurch, won a weekend for two in Stuttgart when she became the millionth visitor to the centre in 1988.

The old Central Library in Trinity Street served Cardiffians well for more than a century. An unofficial protest was staged outside the building by some of the staff over pay and staffing levels planned for the new library in Frederick Street, 1988.

Baths superintentant Mr E.A.
Barnfield chats to 18-year-old
Charles Stacey, who was the first
bather to swim in Roath Park
Lake in seven years, 1957.

Cardiff's first district leisure
centre was the Western Leisure
Centre at Caerau, Ely, which was
opened on 20 July 1978.

The world famous Cardiff Arms Park was the venue for these sheep dog trials which took place on 28 August 1924.

CHAPTER FIFTEEN
Sporting Moments

Cardiff hosted the sixth Empire and Commonwealth Games in 1958 and the athletic events were staged at the Cardiff Arms Park. The Duke of Edinburgh passes through lines of competitors at the close of the games.

Australian Herb Elliott winning the mile race in a time of three minutes and 59 seconds. He beat fellow Australians Merv Lincoln and Albert Thomas.

The English girls, extreme right of picture, set a new world record in the 4 x 110 yards relay of 45.3 seconds.

New Zealander Murray Halberg, winner of the three miles race, receives his gold medal from Mr A.M.C. Jenour. Also on the rostrum are Australia's Albert Thomas (left), who was second, and New Zealander Norman Scott, who was third.

Australia's Marlene Mathews, winner of the 100 yards event, receiving her gold medal. She won by inches from England's Heather Young (left) and Madeline Weston, setting a British all-comers, British National and Empire Games record of 10.6 seconds.

The cycling events were held at Maindy Stadium and Australia's R.F. Ploog (right) won the 1,000 metres scratch sprint, beating England's K. Barton (left). The man wearing sunglasses is the Duke of Edinburgh.

Wales's leading international show jumping competitor, Cardiff-born David Broome, is seen riding Wildfire 111 at the Hobby Horse Showjumping Championships at Ninian Park in 1960.

At the Cardiff Arms Park, Cardiff wing J.H. Williams makes a break after receiving a pass from centre Maurice Richards during the Cardiff v Llanelli match, February 1966.

Cardiff Rugby club touring team arrive at Cardiff General Station after a three-week tour of South Africa, May 1967.

The Taff Swim was originally held in the River Taff from 1924 until it moved to Roath Park Lake in 1931. These female competitors are seen taking the plunge in the 1954 race. The last Taff Swim took place in 1961.

Sixty-five-year-old Martin Richards, of Cardiff, was one of the thousands of runners seen crossing the line in the *Western Mail* Marathon of 1982. Thirty-five years earlier, in 1947, Martin had won the Welsh Marathon Championship, but on that occasion there were only six competitors and four of them failed to complete the course!

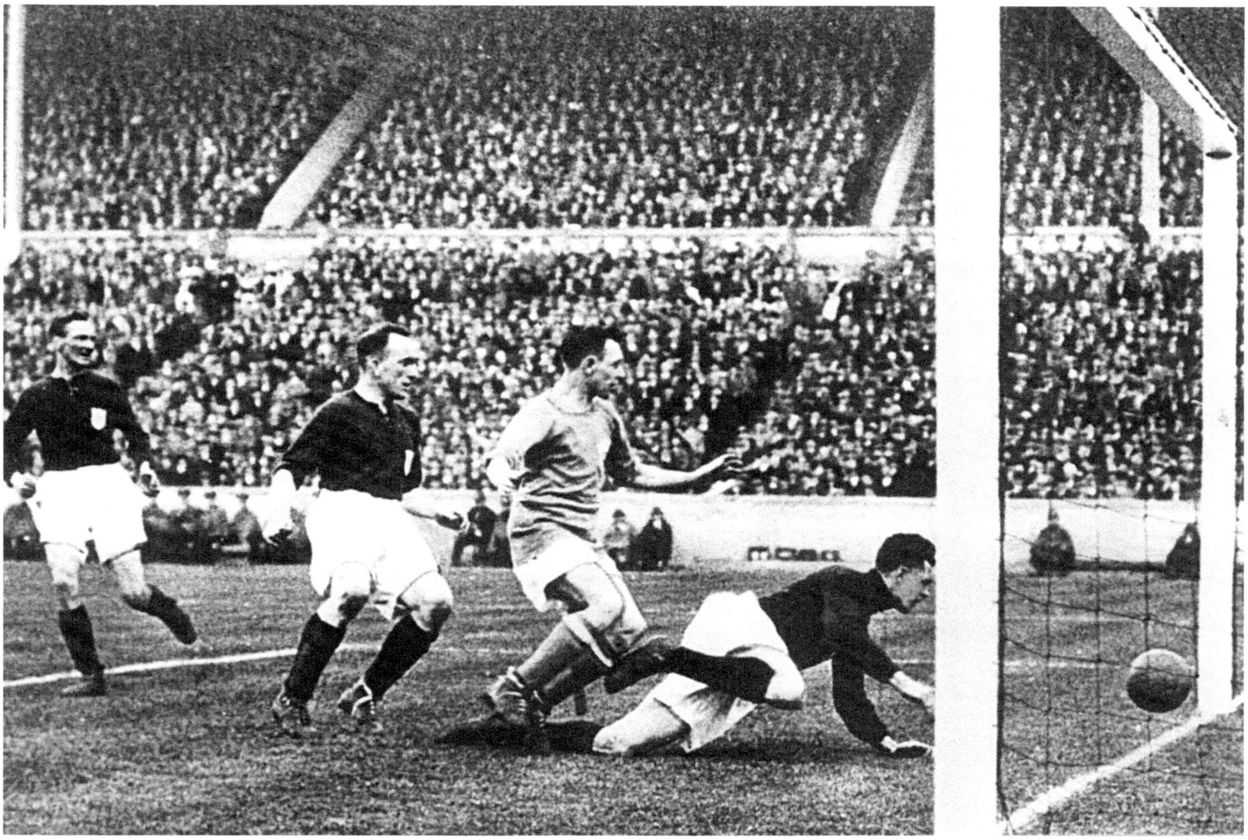

The goal which won the 1927 FA Cup for Cardiff City at Wembley Stadium. Cardiff beat Arsenal 1–0 and Hugh Ferguson was the scorer, but some claim the ball was helped over the line by Len Davies.

Cardiff City Football Club with the FA Cup trophy.

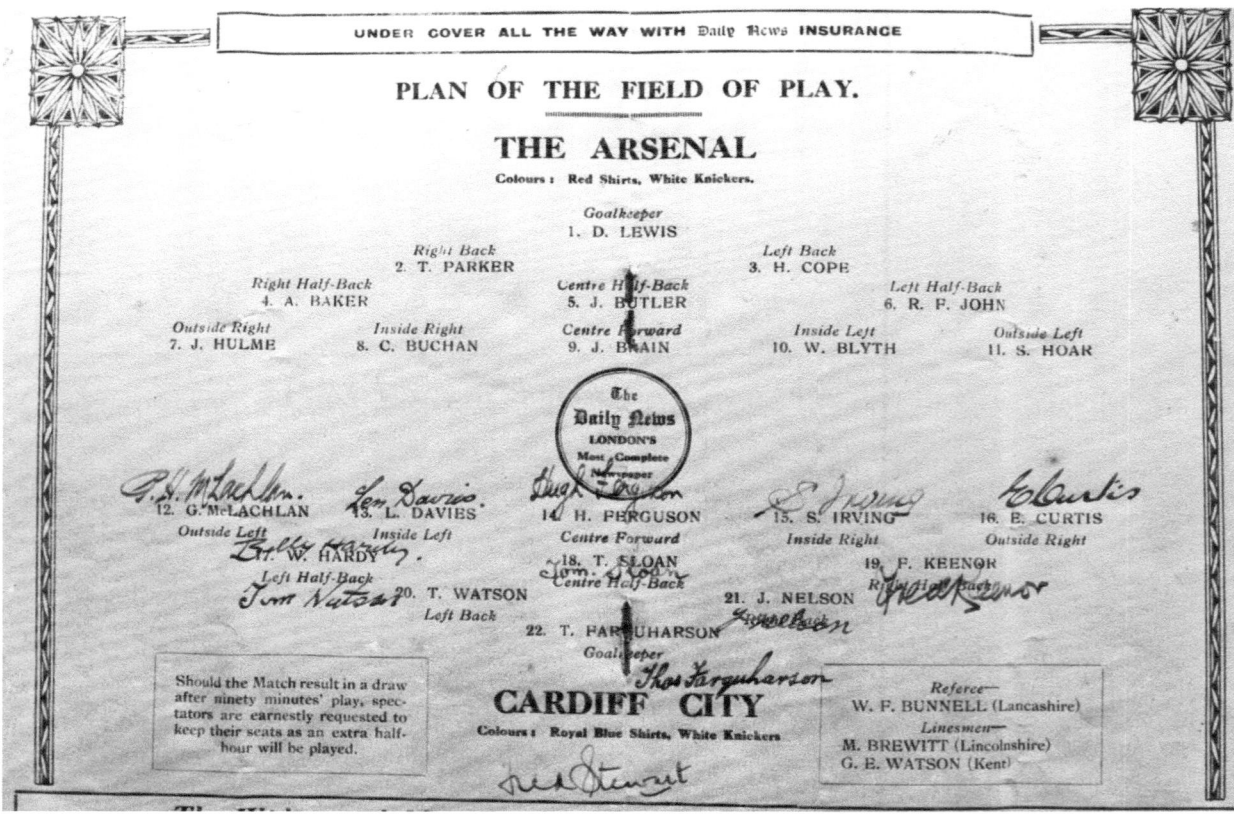

Author/publisher Stewart Williams with former Cardiff City soccer star Ernie Curtis (see introduction).

UNDER COVER ALL THE WAY WITH *Daily News* INSURANCE

PLAN OF THE FIELD OF PLAY.

THE ARSENAL

Colours : Red Shirts, White Knickers.

Goalkeeper
1. D. LEWIS

Right Back
2. T. PARKER

Left Back
3. H. COPE

Right Half-Back
4. A. BAKER

Centre Half-Back
5. J. BUTLER

Left Half-Back
6. R. F. JOHN

Outside Right
7. J. HULME

Inside Right
8. C. BUCHAN

Centre Forward
9. J. BRAIN

Inside Left
10. W. BLYTH

Outside Left
11. S. HOAR

The *Daily News* LONDON'S Most Complete Newspaper

12. G. McLACHLAN
Outside Left

13. L. DAVIES
Inside Left

14. H. FERGUSON
Centre Forward

15. S. IRVING
Inside Right

16. E. CURTIS
Outside Right

17. W. HARDY
Left Half-Back

18. T. SLOAN
Centre Half-Back

19. F. KEENOR

20. T. WATSON
Left Back

21. J. NELSON

22. T. FARQUHARSON
Goalkeeper

CARDIFF CITY

Colours : Royal Blue Shirts, White Knickers.

Should the Match result in a draw after ninety minutes' play, spectators are earnestly requested to keep their seats as an extra half-hour will be played.

Referee—
W. F. BUNNELL (Lancashire)
Linesmen—
M. BREWITT (Lincolnshire)
G. E. WATSON (Kent)

Cardiff City club historian Ceri Stennett's proud possession is a signed programme for the 1927 FA Cup Final, which cost him £120 in 1983.

Cardiff's Ely Racecourse was in a direct line of descent from the old racecourse at Heath Park. Racing was held at Ely from 1855 until 1939. It owed its beginnings to sporting folk such as the Homfrays, the Clays, and the Williamses, who formed the nucleus of the Cardiff Race Club, pictured here on 17 April 1933.

Over the Sticks, Ely Races, 26 May 1927. The grandstand can be seen in the background left of picture.

Members of the Cardiff Race Club at Ely
Races, 28 April 1937.

Cardiff's most famous
boxer was Peerless Jim
Driscoll. When he died in
1925 thousands of people
lined the streets to watch
his funeral procession.

G.V. Wynne-Jones shows a pair of Jim Driscoll's boxing gloves to Olympic long jump gold medallist Lynn Davies;
Allan Bruce, principal of the National Sports Centre; Dewi Griffiths, BBC Wales; Harold Oakes, director Sports
Council for Wales and Olympic Games sprinter Ron Jones. The gloves were donated to the Welsh Sports Hall of
Fame by Michael Hart.

Speedway first came to Cardiff at the Welsh White City Stadium in Sloper Road in 1928. It was revived at the new
Penarth Road Stadium, seen here in 1951.

The Cardiff Dragons Speedway team.

Cardiff Dragons defeated Wolverhampton Wasps at the Penarth Road Stadium in 1952.

New Zealander Mick Holland was a great favourite with the Dragon fans.

Another popular speedway star was Australian Mick Callaghan.